D0428987

READING POWER

Edición CENTRAL

Bilingu

(Record-Breaking Animals)

THE SLOTH
World's Slowest Mammal

El perezoso
El mamífero más lento del mundo

Joy Paige

The Rosen Publishing Group's
PowerKids Press™ & Buenas Letras™
New York

1

Published in 2003 by The Rosen Publishing Group, Inc.
29 East 21st Street, New York, NY 10010
Copyright © 2003 by The Rosen Publishing Group, Inc.

First Bilingual Edition 2003
First Edition in English 2002

Book Design: Michael DeLisio
Photo Credits: Cover, pp. 7, 9, 13, 15 © Animals Animals; pp. 5, 19 © Corbis; pp. 11, 21 © National Geographic; p.17 © Kevin Schafer/Corbis

Paige, Joy
The Sloth: World's slowest mammal/El perezoso: El mamífero más lento del mundo/Joy Paige ; traducción al español: Spanish Educational Publishing
p. cm. — (Record-Breaking Animals)
Includes bibliographical references and index.
ISBN 0-8239-6893-6 (lib. bdg.)
1. Sloths—Juvenile literature. [1. Sloths. 3. Spanish Language Materials—Bilingual.] I. Title.

Printed in The United States of America

Contents

Contenido

Sloths are mammals.
They live in South America
and Central America.

El perezoso es un mamífero.
Vive en América del Sur
y en América Central.

Central America
América Central

South America
América del Sur

5

Sloths like warm weather.

––––––––––––––––

A los perezosos les gustan
los lugares cálidos.

Sloths live in the trees in the forests. They can live in one tree for a long time.

_____

Los perezosos viven
en los árboles.
Viven en un mismo árbol
durante mucho tiempo.

Sloths hide in the trees.
They are the same color as
the trees. This makes them
hard to see.

———————————————

Los perezosos se esconden
en los árboles.
Son del mismo color
que los árboles.
Por eso es difícil verlos.

Sloths hang upside down from the branches of the trees. They eat upside down. They even sleep upside down!

———————————————

Los perezosos se cuelgan
de las ramas de los árboles.
Comen colgados.
¡Hasta duermen colgados!

Sloths sleep during the day.
They sleep 15 hours a day!

Los perezosos duermen de día.
¡Duermen 15 horas al día!

Sloths eat the leaves from the trees. They also eat the fruit.

Los perezosos comen las hojas y los frutos de los árboles.

Sloths cannot walk. When
they come down from the trees,
they pull themselves along
the ground.

———————————

Los perezosos no caminan.
Cuando bajan de los árboles
se arrastran por el suelo.

It can take a whole day for a sloth to move from one tree to another. Sloths are the slowest mammals in the world!

———————

A veces un perezoso
demora todo un día
en ir de un árbol a otro.
¡Los perezosos son
los mamíferos
más lentos del mundo!

Glossary

fruit (**froot**) a juicy product of a tree

leaves (**leevz**) thin green parts of a tree

mammals (**mam**-uhlz) warm-blooded animals

upside down (**uhp**-syd **down**) when what should be on top is on the bottom

Glosario

cálidos lugares de clima templado, de calor moderado

colgarse suspenderse de algo

frutos (los) productos jugosos de los árboles

hojas (las) partes verdes de los árboles

mamífero (el) animal de sangre caliente

Resources / Recursos

Here are more books to read about sloths:
Otros libros que puedes leer sobre el perezoso:

Sloths
S.L. Berry
The Creative Company (1999)

The Upside-Down Sloth
Fay Robinson
Children's Press (1994)

Web sites
Due to the changing nature of Internet links, PowerKids Press has developed an online list of Web sites related to the subject of this book. This site is updated regularly. Please use this link to access the list:

Sitios web
Debido a las constantes modificaciones en los sitios de Internet, PowerKids Press ha desarrollado una guía on-line de sitios relacionados al tema de este libro. Nuestro sitio web se actualiza constantemente. Por favor utiliza la siguiente dirección para consultar la lista:

http://www.buenasletraslinks.com/chl/tmb

Word count in English: 134
Número de palabras en español: 129

Index

Índice